W9-BHS-570

Eid al-Fitr

FESTIVALS AROUND THE WORLD

Grace Jones

AV² provides enriched content that supplements and complements this book. Weigl's AV² books strive to create inspired learning and engage young minds in a total learning experience.

Your AV² Media Enhanced books come alive with...

Audio
Listen to sections of the book read aloud.

Key Words
Study vocabulary, and complete a matching word activity.

Video
Watch informative video clips.

Quizzes
Test your knowledge.

Go to **www.av2books.com,** and enter this book's unique code.

Embedded Weblinks
Gain additional information for research.

Slide Show
View images and captions, and prepare a presentation.

BOOK CODE

L B F 3 5 7 7 4

AV² by Weigl brings you media enhanced books that support active learning.

Try This!
Complete activities and hands-on experiments.

... and much, much more!

Published by AV² by Weigl
350 5ᵗʰ Avenue, 59ᵗʰ Floor   New York, NY 10118
Website: www.av2books.com

Library of Congress Cataloging-in-Publication Data

Names: Jones, Grace, 1990- author.
Title: Eid al-fitr / Grace Jones.
Description: New York, NY : AV2 by Weigl, [2019] I Series: Festivals around the world
Identifiers: LCCN 2018003638 (print) I LCCN 2018004975 (ebook) I ISBN 9781489678096 (Multi User ebook) I ISBN 9781489678072 (hardcover : alk. paper) I ISBN 9781489678089 (softcover)
Subjects: LCSH: Eid al-Fitr--Juvenile literature. I Fasts and feasts--Islam--Juvenile literature.
Classification: LCC BP186.45 (ebook) I LCC BP186.45 .J65 2019 (print) I DDC 297.3/6--dc23
LC record available at https://lccn.loc.gov/2018003638

Printed in the United States of America in Brainerd, Minnesota
1 2 3 4 5 6 7 8 9 0   22 21 20 19 18

032018
120417

Project Coordinator: Heather Kissock   Designer: Ana María Vidal

First published by Book Life in 2017

Weigl acknowledges Getty Images, Alamy, Newscom, Shutterstock, and iStock as the primary image suppliers for this title.

Eid al-Fitr

FESTIVALS AROUND THE WORLD

Contents

Hello, my name is Noor.

When you see Noor, she will tell you how to say a word.

3

What Is a Festival?

A festival takes place when people come together to celebrate a special event or time of the year. Some festivals last for only one day and others can go on for many months.

Some people celebrate festivals by having a party with their family and friends. Others celebrate by holding special events, performing dances or playing music.

Many mosques feature a **large dome** called a **qubba**.

Noor says:
MOSK (Mosque)
KUR-AN (Qur'an)

What Is Islam?

Islam is a religion that began over one thousand years ago in the Middle East. Muslims believe in one God, called Allah, whom they pray to in a mosque or Muslim place of worship.

Muslims read a holy book called the Qur'an. The Qur'an is Allah's word and instructs people on how to practice their faith. An imam teaches people about Allah's word and leads prayers in the mosque.

What is Eid al-Fitr?

Eid al-Fitr is a festival celebrated by Muslims on three days of every year to mark the end of Ramadan. Ramadan is a time when Muslims fast during the daylight hours of an entire month.

Eid al-Fitr means the "Festival of the Breaking Fast" because people stop fasting and are allowed to eat in the daytime.

Noor says:
EED AL-FIH-TRA (Eid al-Fitr)
RAM-A-DAN (Ramadan)

9

The Story of Ramadan and Eid al-Fitr

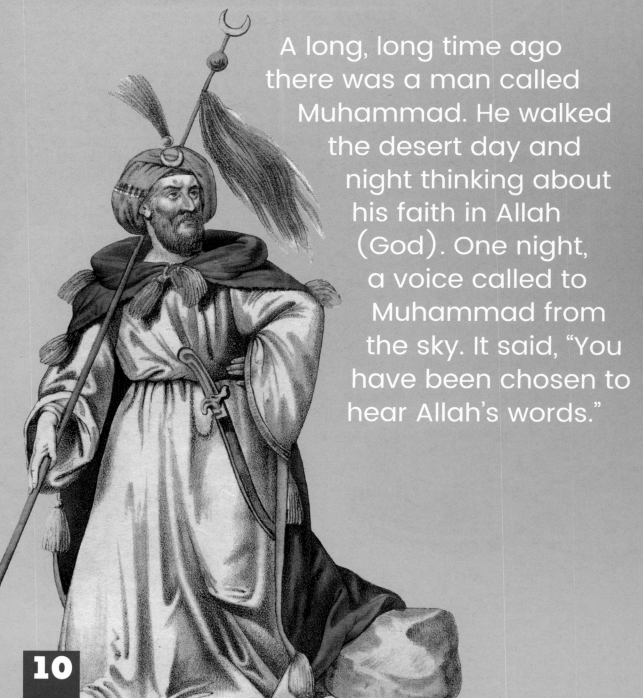

A long, long time ago there was a man called Muhammad. He walked the desert day and night thinking about his faith in Allah (God). One night, a voice called to Muhammad from the sky. It said, "You have been chosen to hear Allah's words."

Allah spoke to Muhammad and told him how to practice his faith and lead a good life. Muhammad spread Allah's words to other people by writing them down in a holy book so all Muslims could follow them. This book was called the Qur'an.

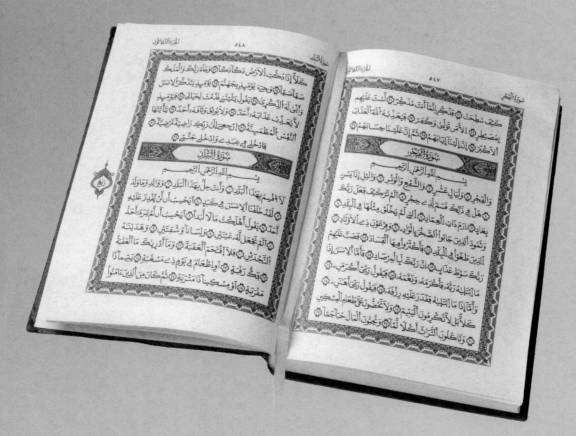

During Eid al-Fitr, people wish each other "**Eid Mubarak**," which means "**happy festival**."

Festival of the Breaking Fast

Muslims believe that it was in the month of Ramadan that Allah passed on his word to Muhammad. To show their love and faith in Allah, they fast for one month. When the new moon comes out, Eid al-Fitr begins and fasting stops.

This is why Eid al-Fitr is also known as the "Festival of the Breaking Fast." It is a time when people eat together, share gifts and spend time with their friends and family.

13

Decorations and Gifts

People dress in their best clothes for Eid al-Fitr. They also decorate their homes with brightly colored balloons, flowers and lights.

Muslim children are often given gifts during Eid al-Fitr. Toys, money and bags of sweets are popular gifts at this time of year.

Prayer and Worship

People go to the mosque very early in the morning to pray. They must wash before going into the mosque as a sign of respect to Allah.

The imam of the mosque holds special prayers for Eid al-Fitr. After prayers finish, everyone continues the celebrations with their family and friends.

Festive Food

Eid al-Fitr is also known as the "Sweet Eid" because of the amount of sweet foods eaten at the festival. A bowl of sweet milk and dates, called sheer khurma, is traditionally eaten for breakfast during Eid.

Noor says:
SHE-ER KUR-MA (Sheer Khurma)
MA-MOO-AL (Ma'amoul)

During the day, other sweet foods, like ma'amoul, are eaten. Ma'amoul are small, round pastries filled with dates, figs or walnuts.

19

Family and Friends

Eid al-Fitr is a time to forgive and share with one another. People give money to others that don't have enough so they can celebrate this special festival too. This is called Zakat al-Fitr.

Although Muslims celebrate their faith in Allah during the festival, Eid al-Fitr is also about spending time with family, friends and loved ones.

Noor says:
ZA-KAT AL-FIH-TRA
(Zakat al-Fitr)

Noor Says . . .

Eid al-Fitr
EED AL-FIH-TRA
Eid al-Fitr is a festival celebrated by Muslims.

Ma'amoul
MA-MOO-AL
Ma'amoul is a bowl of sweet milk and dates eaten at breakfast time during Eid.

Mosque
MOSK
A mosque is a Muslim place of worship.

Qur'an
KUR-AN
The Qur'an is the writing of Allah's word in a holy book.

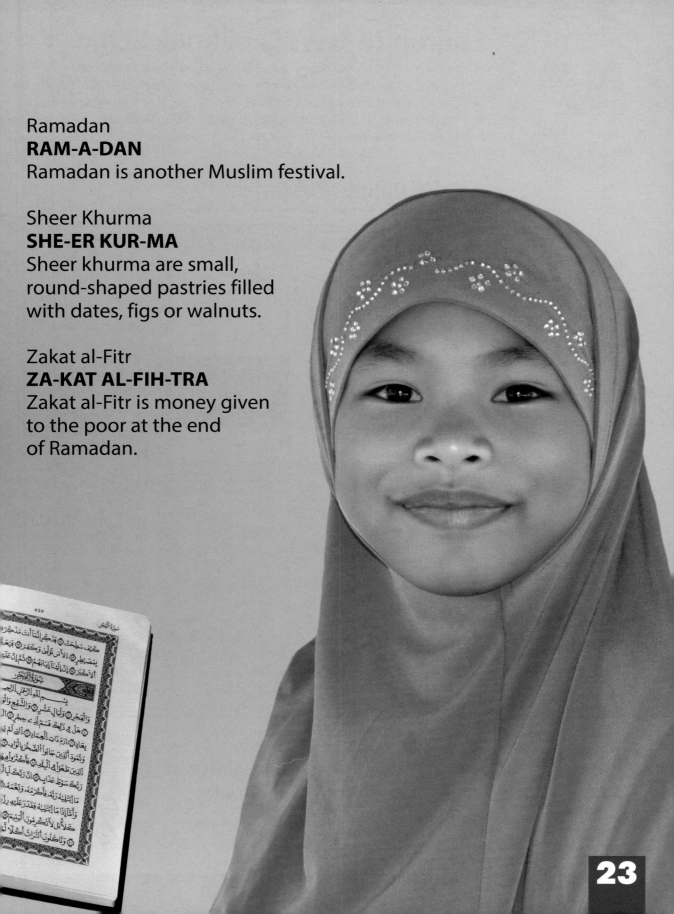

Ramadan
RAM-A-DAN
Ramadan is another Muslim festival.

Sheer Khurma
SHE-ER KUR-MA
Sheer khurma are small,
round-shaped pastries filled
with dates, figs or walnuts.

Zakat al-Fitr
ZA-KAT AL-FIH-TRA
Zakat al-Fitr is money given
to the poor at the end
of Ramadan.

23

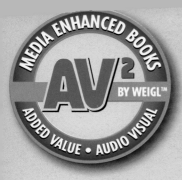

Log on to www.av2books.com

AV² by Weigl brings you media enhanced books that support active learning. Go to www.av2books.com, and enter the special code found on page 2 of this book. You will gain access to enriched and enhanced content that supplements and complements this book. Content includes video, audio, weblinks, quizzes, a slide show, and activities.

AV² Online Navigation

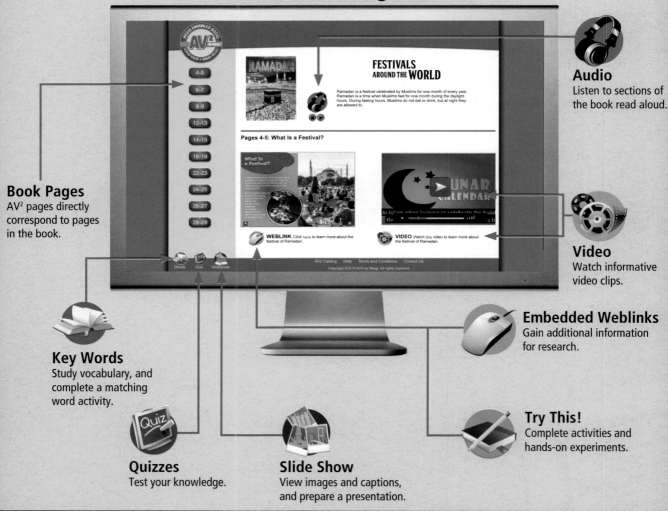

Book Pages
AV² pages directly correspond to pages in the book.

Audio
Listen to sections of the book read aloud.

Video
Watch informative video clips.

Embedded Weblinks
Gain additional information for research.

Key Words
Study vocabulary, and complete a matching word activity.

Quizzes
Test your knowledge.

Slide Show
View images and captions, and prepare a presentation.

Try This!
Complete activities and hands-on experiments.

AV² was built to bridge the gap between print and digital. We encourage you to tell us what you like and what you want to see in the future.

Sign up to be an AV² Ambassador at www.av2books.com/ambassador.